C000212195

This book has been p
with the Christian E
Society has existed since 1870 to present the
fundamental truths of Christianity to enquirers.
Its address is:

1 Little Cloister
Westminster Abbey
London
SW1P 3PL

Other titles in this series:

Why God?

Simon Barrington-Ward

LION PUBLISHING

Copyright © 1993 Simon Barrington-Ward
The author asserts the moral right to be identified as the author of
this work

This edition published in 1997 by Lion Publishing plc Sandy Lane
West, Oxford, England
ISBN 0 7459 3713 6

Albatross Books Pty Ltd PO Box 320, Sutherland, NSW 2232,
Australia
ISBN 0 7324 1588 8

First edition 1997
10 9 8 7 6 5 4 3 2 1 0

Why God?

Why God? How do I begin to answer that question, and from what starting-point? I believe the best way to do it is through the story of a pilgrimage.

My pilgrim is a boy called Christopher, whose story overlaps at a number of points with my own.

A glimpse of wholeness

When Christopher was six he already was aware of some kind of mysterious parent figure over-arching his own parents, a figure to whom they also, in some strange way,

5

looked for safety and guidance. He was used to the reassuring rhythm of the nightly prayers his mother said with him. He went occasionally to Sunday school and listened to stories, drew, and sang.

But one day he was taken right out of London, where they lived, to some bluebell woods, somewhere in Kent. He stepped out of the coach into the wood where already others were wading out into an ocean of flowers. And quite suddenly he was transfixed.

It was as though the film stopped and the figures stayed, their movements suspended. Through the moist, translucent leaves, the dark pillars of the tree trunks, the scattered shafts of light, the receding waves of intense blue, something overwhelming touched him at the very core.

He felt suddenly as if he was being brought into oneness with everything, everyone, the landscape and the figures. He experienced each detail as part of some great whole in which he too had his special place.

Each person became truly themselves and all of them belonged to each other. The whole scene was drawn into one indivisible whole.

Then, a voice was suddenly calling his name. With difficulty, and even pain, he came back. Slowly he returned to the surface of the ordinary, broken world. But he was touched with an unforgettable trace of that inmost awareness, even though for a long time he would not have been able to put it into words nor express more than a fraction of what it meant. Occasionally, some new encounter would stir a memory of that moment of insight. But for the most part it left Christopher with a sense of absence. It was as though a door had shut and there was no re-entry.

There are, in fact, centres where research is being carried out into such experiences. It seems almost as if those who undergo them find themselves reaching out beyond the particular cultural setting which made the experience itself possible and recognisable. For Christopher, as for doubtless many others, every subsequent phase of his journey was an attempt to find a way back through to the unity in diversity he knew he had glimpsed.

A rational vision

The most important step in the years which followed was Christopher's entry into the classroom of a great schoolmaster, a man whose vision was to dominate his early youth. Entering Dr Addison's classroom was rather like walking into a cathedral. You were met by a reverent hush and suddenly you realized that it was because the great man was already there when you arrived, brooding over his desk like a cloud on Sinai, his great, grey, leonine head bent over his writing. A voice from all around you would somehow reverberate as the words sounded softly but strongly, 'Close the door!' The appointed pupil would then step forward, like an acolyte carrying out an essential rite. Then the lesson began.

Dr Addison was a scientist who taught Philosophy and English and was something of a phenomenon. What he focused upon first and foremost in the periods given to Religious Knowledge was 'how do we *know* what is true?' He liked to start with optical illusions, like the famous black and white picture which can either be two faces looking at one another or a white urn set on a black ground. He wanted to show the children that even seeing the world around us is much more complicated than we think. Our senses do not give us a direct picture of the world. Instead, our mind is all the time making choices and decisions. It is like an artist or a scientist, selecting and organizing from all the mass of material available to us. Out of the flood of light waves and sound waves we encounter, we simply make a tiny selection of those that seem significant to us and group and arrange them so as to make sense of them.

Sometimes, as the pictures he put before the children showed, it is quite difficult for our brain and senses to decide. In other words, we are all the time searching for the best interpretation of the data which we choose to give attention to. We are constantly arriving at a theory as to what is there and then putting our faith in it. We make the best bet and normally find that it more or less works. What our senses are constantly doing is arranging what they pick out into a theory or a hypothesis and then by an act of faith we entrust ourselves to it. So you can say that in a real sense, believing is seeing. An optical illusion or an hallucination occurs when our perceptual theory turns out to be wrong.

Of course we are enormously helped in this process by our nurture and education. We grow up into a way of seeing the world which we learn from those around us from our earliest childhood. We enter into the body of theory which they have already built up. Indeed, the very language which we learn to speak divides the world up for us and gives us the way of looking at the world in which we early learn to put our trust.

Dr Addison suggested that we are rather like scientists, who start their students off by teaching them to take hold of and use the body of theory which their elders have already built up. They are initiated into this body of theory. But then they begin to find that there are certain points at which these theories don't fit the evidence so well.

There may even be large gaps and questions which the theory doesn't seem to cope with. So they start to brood over these problem areas until perhaps the theory itself seems to break down. There must be another better way of grouping and relating the evidence. In this search, the new pattern sometimes seems to dawn like a revelation. Indeed many great discoveries originate in a simple shape or image which begins to suggest to the scientist a whole new theory.

It makes sense of things, and even though none of the experimental evidence is yet clear, the scientist has a hunch that this new pattern is going to work. There are famous examples like, of course, the double helix through which Francis Crick and Jim Watson arrived at the structure of the DNA molecule.

What appeals about the pattern which we then put our faith in is that it is often so amazingly simple and also provides an attractive way of arranging the evidence. The most compelling theory or hypothesis may even be described by the scientist as 'beautiful' or 'elegant', as when Watson said of the double helix that it was 'too pretty not to be true'!

So this was the way in which Dr Addison introduced Christopher and his friends to what he called the *coherence* theory of truth. It was the pattern which made the best sense of things and gave the greatest sense of completeness and which seemed to *fit* all the evidence by which we could test it, the pattern that was at least *nearest* the truth. On such a pattern scientists may stake years of time and energy and effort. They may even risk giving their whole lifetime to it. In the end, this has to be an act of faith.

Dr Addison described faith as 'the resolution to stand or fall by the truest theory', that is to say the theory that selects and arranges all the evidence best.

By this time, the children were really gripped and fascinated. Addison could easily be imitated and they used to go round copying his way of talking about the 'coheerence' theory of truth. But they loved him and were really excited by what he had shown them.

What science presents us with is some kind of an emerging order out of the chaos of existence itself. From the moment of the 'big bang' with which it all began, the wonderful body of theory which physicists have arrived at suggests that we are part of an immensely rich, dynamic, unfolding order. Of course there is terrific variety and complexity disclosed in an incredible network of processes. Much of it seems incomplete and open and full of mystery.

Yet space, time, matter and energy are all integrally related in an evolving whole.

And, what is more exciting, the whole universe seems from its start to provide the unique conditions which can lead to the eventual appearance of human consciousness. Even to understand the physical basis of the world properly is to understand the essence of human beings themselves. We seem to be the point at which the universe becomes conscious of itself. And everything about its essential constituents from the beginning seems to have prepared the way for our appearance.

'Now what,' Dr Addison asked, 'is the *theoria* (a Greek word meaning vision, he explained) or theory which can best interpret this whole amazing story?'

He believed that the world's religions, from the beginning, at their greatest and best at least, have provided such a *theoria*. They have offered to the societies in which they develop a picture of how the world works, a theory of the universe.

This is larger scale than most scientific theories, of course, because it covers all aspects of our life and of the way things are. It includes religious experience, experience of beauty and moral experience, the experience of good and bad. It seeks to answer questions about why anything is and to interpret, guide and underpin every aspect of our life.

What Dr Addison argued is that religion as a whole still offers human beings the most completely satisfying and coherent interpretation of their whole existence. That is why we can stake ourselves on it being true. It genuinely offers us the most convincing arrangement of all the evidence and the most profound and attractive hypothesis.

To suggest that all this came about by chance is to offer a theory which is seemingly less probable and which in a way contradicts the whole assumption and instinct of science itself.

Addison loved to show his pupils how, as we push beyond the physical world, our minds keep asking what underlies our theorizing. We keep pressing further in and deeper until we arrive at the insight that only an ultimate, necessary, divine Being *could* be the ground of everything.

This is what the great religions have always claimed. Here, Dr Addison said he was talking about all the great world faiths, Hinduism, Buddhism, Judaism, Islam and Christianity. He would read aloud from their different scriptures and thinkers. Sometimes he seemed to be summing them all up as different versions, different forms, of the same central Reality, the one God or Absolute. This reality could be well hidden behind their different particular emphases of tradition or practice. Sometimes he pictured the religions more as complementary, each religion emphasizing a different aspect of the same deep-laid set of values in the universe. These values, truth, goodness, beauty, happiness and wisdom, are all aspects of the supreme Spirit, on which different religions in the end converge.

Dr Addison was a great believer in prayer. He felt that the kind of world which the scientists are showing us now is so much more complex and open than the old mechanical picture which Victorian science used to suggest; that there is much more room for human observers to share in its shaping. Even scientific experiments themselves touch on it and change it. But increasingly our universe seems not only deeply understandable, it also appears to be a delicately interdependent network of events. 'Touch it in one place and another trembles.' So an incident as tiny as a thought could conceivably set processes in motion in a way we still may not fully understand.

Christopher and his friends were generally excited and inspired by Addison's picture of a world grounded in God and by his claim that this is the supreme theory, *theoria* or vision which can grasp our minds and hearts.

But he had one last, crucial, separate argument which he seemed to bring in almost on its own at the end. He used to say that human beings have found a deep urge within them to decide upon a moral order. There seems to be some kind of pressure upon us driving us all the time to try to discern what is good and to seek to realize that. Different societies and, increasingly today, different people may have varied in their understanding of exactly what that goodness involved. But in the end, and certainly in our own day, religions and societies seem to be converging more and more in their definition of the great moral values. Now, not only does our *rational* order require a necessary divine ground and source, a God on whom all depends for its being, a God who cannot fail to be eternally there and who can ultimately be depended upon, but also our *moral* order needs that kind of foundation.

You can't keep your moral values alive within an on-going community if they have no final ground of this kind.

Take away the spiritual basis and morality becomes, in the end, just a matter of personal preference, either of individuals or of societies. You may keep your moral values going for a bit but if they do not rest on some deeper foundation than mere human choice, they will be rapidly weakened. All rational attempts to justify morality as a mere human practice without any spiritual basis have failed.

The most powerful alternative theory has been put forward by some biologists who maintain that morality and, indeed, belief in God and thus religions themselves, arise merely out of the evolutionary need for self-preservation. Religions enhance human survival. That is why they have flourished.

But this, Addison argued, is a far less coherent and elegant theory than the religious alternative. It requires far more intricate ingenuity and special pleading to argue that all ethical and spiritual frameworks are the mere product of a biological process. Any theory that reduces everything to such a simple cause is always forced to exclude too much of our experience.

The final and most daunting objection to Dr Addison's case was, of course, the existence of evil and suffering. The children raised this quite fiercely and argued passionately.

But Dr Addison, even though he himself suffered permanently from illness and pain, strongly maintained his conviction that, as he would put it, 'all is well in the best of all possible (next) worlds'!

He claimed that God had to limit himself if he was to create a world in which free personal beings like us could emerge. For this to happen, there had to be an element of chance and choice in the universe and an interplay from the beginning of order and chaos. We must be fully free to shape our own lives. God can work with us and in us to transfigure the tragic suffering that results from this free play of things. But, in the end, if the unique types of good which we find in this world of ours are to be realized, then this appalling pain is the apparent cost of it. We seem only able to arrive at unselfish love, or beauty, truth or goodness, through experiencing hatred, ugliness, falsehood and evil. We can only trust that we will discover beyond this life that it has all been worth while. Even in our experience of this life we have, as we struggle to learn and grow, through light and shadow, an inkling of that final realization. Even our greatest works of art point us to that.

Descent into the subjective

Thus 'The Maestro', as they called him, presented Christopher and his friends with their *theoria*, his rational vision. It was powerful and indeed it sustained Christopher through university and through some desultory church-going and seemed to offer him a satisfactory framework for life. The fact that it was somewhat abstract and individualistic, an armchair philosophy comfortably defending the status quo, did not really trouble Christopher.

It might have continued so had he not been jerked out of his rather insulated life in Britain, to go and take up a post in the Free University in the then still-ruined city of Berlin. He found himself suddenly thrown from his armchair into a considerable turmoil.

Christopher was staggered by the Berlin of that time.

As the aircraft banked and descended over the city on a grey, misty autumn day he gazed down on a moon landscape. There were crumbled mounds of masonry and fingers of shattered tower blocks. There were hollow façades, lines of windows into daylight, ruins to the horizon. The Wall had not been built yet, but Christopher could see the clear outline of the Brandenburg Gate looking like an entrance from nowhere into nowhere.

When he arrived at the house in the suburbs where he was to live, the door was opened by his fellow-lodger, one Hans Baedeker, one of the most extraordinary people he had ever met.

Hans was thin, tall, sensitive and fine-drawn. He was a pale, nervous young man who spoke with great intensity. He had been, as a schoolboy, part of Hitler's last defence of Berlin. Then he had been a prisoner of the Americans. Finally he had gone back to his home in the East, before fleeing to West Berlin. Now he was immersed in Business Studies. He was engrossed in the study of the so-called 'German Miracle', the rise of a new capitalist economy. He would hold forth to Christopher on how six powerful people were shaping that economy through their vast monopolies. It was a thought that fascinated him.

The two of them ate supper together every evening. As the conversation turned to philosophy of life, Hans soon gave himself to demolishing Christopher's cherished ideas. He sought to reduce them to the same kind of ruins that not far away stretched for miles. Indeed, one day they went for a walk through piles of rubble. Hans pointed out how the wreckage of the city heaped in piles about them contained fragments of all the varied styles of architecture from every epoch of history, not only European but Babylonian, Egyptian, Indian and Islamic. 'We shall soon rebuild,' he said in his strangely rapid, grating voice, 'but we mustn't forget that what we see here is the reality. We have to learn to look at all human beliefs, ideologies, convictions, institutions, as an auctioneer looks at works of art. They are all just products of particular human situations. They are nothing more.'

For Hans, the world was just one gigantic market. And that went for all its theories and visions and values too. They were all just the products of different societies. They were different ways of looking at things being purveyed by different groups.

When Christopher tried to expound to him the grand picture Dr Addison had presented and the coherence theory of truth, Hans was quite dismissive. 'Of course,' he would say, 'your schoolmaster,' as he called him, 'was right in saying that all we can do is to construct our theories. Even what we perceive with our senses is already theory laden. As somebody said, "There are no facts, only interpretations." But where he was wrong was in clinging on to the idea that there is some objective reality out there and there is some theory which is closer to that reality than any other.'

Christopher then asked him about the general picture of the universe which was emerging through scientists today.

Hans would have none of it. 'All we have in science,' he said, 'is a series of rival research programmes, each shaping its own pattern. Some may produce more effective-seeming hypotheses than others and may become powerful for a time, but the outcome is never finally settled. The majority of scientists may be convinced for a time but it will only be a fashion.' This, too, was basically a market-place where the theories that seemed to work best could prevail temporarily. 'It's the same with all philosophies and religions,' he said. 'No *one* could be shown to be more compelling than another. They are all ways of ordering our experience and giving our lives a meaningful direction. But beyond them there is no actual objective reality. All we have is an endless flux of pictures, voices, fantasies, dreams, which we create from within ourselves.'

He paused. 'If you like, I could say,' and he waved his arms dramatically round in an all-embracing gesture, 'I myself am god. The god out there is dead, but then in a way so am I. "I" also am just a creation of my own. Psychiatrists have shown that each one of us is no more than a mass of contradictions. We ourselves, as well as our worlds, are just ingenious fictions partly produced by our society, partly by each one of us. People like your schoolmaster just try to impose on us one view of reality. They are authoritarians. They are like those people across there who run East Berlin. There can be no one theory of the whole. There is no whole. Just a plurality of theories. A mass of possibilities. They are as empty and meaningless as these piles of rubble until we arrange them in our own patterns.'

Their last argument was about morality. Here, Hans was sharply insistent that there was no ground for morality outside the particular choices of individuals or societies. 'When you say something is true, or is good, you are simply expressing a personal preference. It cannot be rationalized further convincingly.'

In the face of this sceptical assault Christopher fell silent.

Hans had a sister, an equally intense and articulate girl called Gretel. In a strange way she was very like him. But she had long golden hair and dressed in flowing cottons with huge shapeless sweaters and beads. She was a kind of forerunner of the hippies. She lived in a commune of students who meditated and ate vegetarian food. She told Christopher not to listen to Hans. She said that his philosophy was the final sink of nothingness into which reason drains when it becomes so self-absorbed. For all that, she and her brother were very close. Christopher went round to visit the commune. He sat in their meditation room where they kept up a monotonous recitation of the word 'om', a Hindu word for God.

Gretel tried to convince Christopher that 'the heart has reasons which the mind has not'. Perhaps that was why Hans called her 'the last Romantic'. She wanted Hans to feel the invisible, inner dimension of all life. There is an inner reality, she claimed, which you can explore in your own being. She wanted him to get in touch with an inner energy that was to be reached not by the reason but with the imagination, so he could get rid of repression and fear. She and her friends were in touch with a new 'dynamic', a new 'potential', which linked them up with the natural world. It was this world that we had tortured with our technology and wounded with our wars. Their worship and meditation evoked an amazing medley of spiritual beings. They talked about mystical techniques to discover the divine spark within us and to release it. They were awaiting the final dawning of total healing, joy and fulfilment, in a kind of spiritual Utopia. It was all strongly individualistic. Each person must live their own reality. They loved to quote Hermann Hesse, 'Every life stands beneath its own star.'

The members of the commune were certainly kind and gentle, but a little abstracted. It was almost as if each of them were living her or his own dream. All shared a sense of breaking away, up beyond the ruins, in a soaring quest for a higher order of existence. They looked for humanity to rise above evil by its own spiritual flight, wheeling and weaving its way with the synchronization of a flock of birds.

They were full of tranquil, rather passive, expectation, looking for a new synthesis of all the religions to which Great Souls like Christ, Buddha, Muhammed, Ramakrishna, and other such had pointed the way. New powers would be released. The femininity in us all would be set free, as we made contact with the Inner Divinity, a Higher Intelligence, an ultimate God-consciousness to which our own self is both the path and the goal. There was certainly an intoxicating sense of some aspect of reality which Hans had neglected.

Christopher stepped out into the light of day, the 'Om' still vibrating through him and the discussion of life forces, cosmic principles, self-realization and the unifying centre still ringing in his ears. But he had a strong sense of returning to a struggle inside him and around him which really had to be reckoned with. He was coming back into a world where there were no transcendent shortcuts. Instead of being disappointed at this, he was surprised to find himself relieved.

Gretel's last words seemed to sum up the quality in this group which he reacted against. 'We must become artists and scientists of our own lives.' It might have been her brother speaking. It was in this complete dependence on your own self that she was extraordinarily similar to him. Their approaches were like two sides of the same coin. The rationalist and the romantic both ended up in the same cul-de-sac.

A way through the ways

Christopher returned to the house to find an unexpected visitor, a certain Frau Engel, who had called to invite him to a poetry reading in a nearby house later that week. He accepted, drawn by her genuine warmth and kindness, and found himself, to his own surprise, in the house of the local pastor, Pastor Treulicht, and his wife.

A fascinating group of neighbours were gathered there. They formed a cross-section of the local community, ranging from the assistant at the delikatessen and a waiter from the restaurant, to doctors and teachers, secretaries and commuters of all kinds.

Through the discussion on the poetry and then through the Bible studies which unexpectedly followed the week after, Christopher found himself being drawn to this group. What struck him about them from the first was their evident humility and mutual honesty, a kind of trustfulness, vulnerability and openness which attracted him greatly. When he tried to describe it he found himself using the word 'forgiveness'. Indeed, through this group he did himself experience an increasing sense of being accepted, forgiven and deeply cherished. Each further meeting of the group became a kind of home-coming.

This was a community which gave you a feeling of wholeness, of the possibility of a right ordering of your own life and that of society. He felt himself at once encouraged and appreciated. Later, he found he could call it being loved and healed. At the same time as those in the group worked with the refugees, cared for the poor, went to social welfare offices or to political meetings, they struggled with the issues confronting people in the divided city. They looked beyond East and West, Marxism and Capitalism. Their way of life opened the possibility of a new human social order, a new 'city', in which worship, work and leisure, politics, art and life, would all be integrated. Individual freedom and mutual care would form part of the same essential unity in diversity.

Yet there was no hint that they or their society had yet arrived. The essential rhythm was rather one of constant repentance and forgiveness. There was at least one ex-Nazi in the group who could speak freely about his past and who was here fully accepted and thus ready to acknowledge his own wrong.

These people, in their personal struggles, in their relationships with each other, in their social and political action, in their whole understanding of life, were all clearly conscious of continuing failure and the need to change. They were always ready to start again, drawing into the new endeavour insights from the past.

At the centre of this community, Christopher recognized a quality of death and resurrection, of breaking down and building up. He realized that there was one personal centre which drew together all the particular activities of each of the community's members. There was one all-embracing movement, that of the dying of Jesus on his cross and of his rising again. They would all claim to be participating in his life through death. His Spirit, they said, was at work in each of them and among them. They found themselves in him becoming part of a universal redemptive movement at work in the heart of the world.

As Christopher talked with Pastor

Treulicht one evening, he began to see that all the stages through which he had passed were steps on the way into this movement.

Dr Addison had opened up the possibility of a spiritual vision of life today. What he had set before his pupils was still somehow too much of an abstract rationalization. It was too far from the actual personal and social struggles of ordinary life. It had left Christopher with an unknown God, an unknown self, and a largely unknown goal. Hans Baedeker was right in seeing the flaws and illusions in all such perceptions and theories. But he was trapped in his own isolated individuality. His arrogant market philosophy had blinded him to the possibility of there being any genuine growth or development in our grasp upon reality.

Gretel and her community were right in

their aspiration towards some kind of re-shaping of the world. They were surely right in their feeling for some kind of universal movement. But because they were rooted only in their own self-directed fantasy, it turned out to be deceptive. They weren't really grappling with the moral and social realities of themselves or of their society.

But here in this community in Christ, Christopher had met with a real 'Way' in which reality grasps us and we in turn begin to lay hold upon it. First he had been given an experience of the possibility of wholeness through being loved and forgiven from beyond himself. Then came an unmistakable sense of shared moral and intellectual repentance leading to personal and corporate growth. Our theories and perceptions, like our societies and our inmost selves, have to be tested, corrected and re-made. Even our science truly progresses through the same kind of growth through failure, so long as it is set within a community of learning. The physical world it reveals is also a kind of constant, precarious emergence of order out of chaos.

Within a community of forgiveness Christopher could freely recognize the partial nature of all our truths. All our religions and philosophies fail and are broken. But out of the ruins the Cross of Christ perennially points the way to the raising up of a new structure forever needing to be, in turn, broken down and re-shaped. And this redemptive *process*, this pilgrimage of life through death, or of losing life to find it, is the way in which we are truly enabled to participate in the work of the Spirit.

As they sat talking, Christopher found himself gazing at the crucifix on the wall, between two windows. Beyond it he could see the garden outside and the apple trees now just beginning to blossom. Something of this glimpse recalled the bluebell wood and that strange growing feeling that

'The end of all our exploring
Is to arrive where we first started
And see the place for the first time.'

A door that had seemed shut had opened and a way was unfolding which ran through Dr Addison's classroom, Hans's tour of the ruins and Gretel's commune, and which, through the community of the Cross, stretched ahead.

Why God? Because through all our partial theories and visions, we sense, in the end, a moral and spiritual and social wholeness which seems to reach out to us, to touch us, to beckon us on. And we become aware also of our own responsible need, in communion with that crucified and risen Figure, both to receive love and healing and to reach out in turn in a shared movement of continuing failing and finding again, correction and re-direction. We find our meaning in this movement, this inward and outward journey, and through it we discern the nature of what we have come to call Spirit, and God. The Living God is the source, the theme, the rhythm and the goal of this movement, into which humankind is forever being drawn.